V *New Zealand in* IETNAM

General Series No. 5

*This book is dedicated to
Ellen, Jessica, Pia, Caroline and Lillian,
in the hope that theirs may be a better world*

New Zealand in Vietnam

A Study of the Use of Force in International Law

RUPERT GRANVILLE GLOVER

Barrister and Solicitor of the High Court of New Zealand
Lecturer in International Law
University of Canterbury

© Rupert Granville Glover and The Dunmore Press, 1986

First published in 1986
by
The Dunmore Press Limited
PO Box 5115
Palmerston North
New Zealand

ISBN 0 86469 058 4

Printed by Kerslake, Billens and Humphrey Limited

Copyright. No part of this publication may be reproduced, stored in a retrieval system, or transmitted, in any form or by any means, electronic, mechanical photocopying, recording, or otherwise, without the prior written permission of the publishers. Infringements will lead to prosecution.

Contents

Preface		7
Chapter One:	The Background to the War	9
Chapter Two:	New Zealand's Intervention	13
	1. New Zealand's decision to intervene	13
	2. The American attitude to SEATO members	18
	3. The Canberra viewpoint	23
	4. Reluctant escalation	25
Chapter Three:	The Role of SEATO in Vietnam	27
	1. The genesis of SEATO	27
	2. The SEATO Treaty and New Zealand's Approach	29
Chapter Four:	Collective Self-defence in International Law	35
	1. The notion of collective self-defence	35
	2. State practice before the UN Charter	38
	3. The UN Charter and collective self-defence	39
	4. Collective defence and regional arrangements	43
	5. SEATO and the duty to defend	47
Chapter Five:	The Vietnam War: Civil or International?	50
Chapter Six:	Conclusions	53
Abbreviations		58
Notes		59
Index		67

Preface

Much has been written about the war in Vietnam. In particular the legality, both internationally and constitutionally, of the role of the United States in that conflict has been subjected to intense scrutiny. It is not my aim to duplicate that work. Rather my intention has been to examine the small part played, perhaps reluctantly and often controversially, by New Zealand in that war, and by means of this case study to examine the use of force in international law.

There is scarcely an aspect of this war which has not given rise to fundamental disagreements among international lawyers. Many of these questions will be raised in the following chapters. Was Vietnam one state or two? Was the war international or civil? How binding were the Geneva Accords? Attempts will be made to answer these questions and others. But that is not the primary purpose of this book.

My main aim has been to contribute to the literature in international law on the use of force by states, and to do this by means of a case study. My purpose has not been to draw firm conclusions about the legality of New Zealand's involvement in the Vietnam War, although some inevitably emerge. Instead I hope to give an insight into the complex world of international law and politics.

Chapter One sketches briefly the background to the Vietnam War. Chapter Two narrows the field and concentrates on New Zealand's decision to become involved. This chapter is based largely on statements made by the New Zealand Government in parliamentary debates and elsewhere, and on the Pentagon Papers. The latter make surprisingly few overt references to New Zealand, but American attitudes in general to the participation of South-East Asia Treaty Organisation countries can be seen. Australian influences are also considered. Chapter Three deals with the origins of the Organisation, its nature, and attitudes to the Treaty. Chapter Four relates all the foregoing to general principles of international law, and Chapter Five examines briefly the question of whether the war was international or civil. Chapter Six contains my conclusions on the legality of New Zealand's participation in the war in a combat role.

As in so many contentious areas of international law, the question of participation in the Vietnam War carries with it a heavy political component. It may not please some that I have given this component considerable weight in the first half of the book. I can only reply that international law has evolved in many respects as the little sister of international politics. When it is successful, it is often for political reasons. When it fails, politics are usually blamed. And in dealing with a subject so fraught with difficulties as the Vietnam War, evidence tends to be distorted by opinion, and opinion itself tends to be polarised. Conscious of the difficulties, I have attempted to tread carefully and objectively. This study should be regarded as preliminary rather than definitive. However, I hope it will serve as a useful introduction to some of the legal questions which arise when a small nation enters a war on someone else's behalf. While I have aimed my work at students of international law, I have attempted to make it easily comprehensible for the general reader.

As usual, there are many people to whom acknowledgments are due. Professor K.J. Keith of Victoria University of Wellington kindly read the manuscript and offered learned guidance, as did Professor Keith Jackson and Mr Richard Kennaway of the Department of Political Science of the University of Canterbury. Professors John Burrows, Gerald Orchard and John Farrar of the University of Canterbury have encouraged and supported me in my efforts to extend the study of international law within our Faculty. Liz Dobson and David Rowe mastered the intricacies of the word-processor which assembled my text. And Margaret Sewell helped to clarify my thoughts by discussing the manuscript with me throughout its several drafts. To all these people I wish to express my gratitude, while emphasising that any errors or shortcomings in the text are entirely my own.

Rupert Granville Glover
Faculty of Law
University of Canterbury
August 1985.

1 The Background to the War

On 8 June 1965 the Soviet Ambassador in Wellington addressed a statement to the Prime Minister and Minister of External Affairs of New Zealand. The statement noted the announcement by the New Zealand Government on 27 May that it intended to send an artillery battery to support the Australians in what the Ambassador described as 'the aggressive war of the United States of America against the people of Viet Nam'. On 14 June the Soviet Permanent Representative to the United Nations requested the President of the Security Council to circulate the Soviet protest as a document of the Security Council.[1] On 11 June, New Zealand responded to the Soviet note, justifying its decision to enter the Vietnam War in a combat role, and this note in turn was submitted to the Security Council on 16 June 1965.[2]

This exchange of notes brought New Zealand squarely into the arena of international scrutiny for participating in what has proved to be one of the most controversial wars of the twentieth century.

The background to the war in Vietnam is well known. Vietnam was one of three provinces of French Indo-China. Occupied by the Japanese during the Second World War, it was liberated in the South by the British and in the North by the Chinese. In early 1946 French authorities returned. When they attempted to re-occupy the North they found it already in the hands of the Communists. Attempts were made to reach an agreement, but within a year major fighting had broken out. In the North the Viet Minh set themselves up as the Democratic Republic of Vietnam and were soon accorded recognition as the Government by the Soviet Union and the People's Republic of China. The French made an effort to counter the

Communists' inroads by constituting Vietnam an Associate State inside the French Union. The United Kingdom, the United States, and other countries were prompt to recognise the new State, even though its Government had very tenuous control over anything other than the major southern cities.

The war continued, a hybrid between a civil war and a struggle for national liberation by the Viet Minh against the French, until, in 1954, France, the United States, the Soviet Union and the United Kingdom proposed a Geneva Conference to deal with the problems in both Korea and Indo China.

The Conference began on the day that the French forces were decisively defeated and forced to surrender at Dien Bien Phu. An Agreement on the Cessation of Hostilities in Vietnam was drawn up which provided for 'a provisional military demarcation line'[3] to follow approximately the seventeenth parallel. Viet Minh forces were to regroup to the north, and the French to the south. The agreement also established a demilitarised zone of up to five kilometres on either side of the line.[4] A political solution to the conflict was anticipated by providing for general elections to unify the country.[5] From the date of the entry into force of the Agreement the introduction of any troop reinforcements or additional military personnel into Vietnam was prohibited.[6] Similar prohibitions applied to other military activities[7], and the establishment of foreign military bases on either side of the line was expressly proscribed.[8] An International Control Commission, comprising representatives of India (presiding), Canada and Poland, was set up to supervise the implementation of the terms of the Agreement.[9]

The Geneva Conference ended with a Final Declaration which stated that

> ... so far as Viet Nam is concerned, the settlement of political problems, effected on the basis of respect for the principles of independence, unity and territorial integrity, shall permit the Vietnamese people to enjoy the fundamental freedoms, guaranteed by democratic institutions established as a result of free general elections by secret ballot. In order to ensure that sufficient progress in the restoration of peace has been made, and that all the necessary conditions obtain for free expression of the national will,

general elections shall be held in July 1956, under the supervision of an international commission comprised of representatives of the member states of the International Supervisory Commission, referred to in the Agreement on the cessation of hostilities.[10]

This statement seems unequivocal enough. But it has been pointed out that it is doubtful whether the Final Declaration amounted to a treaty creating binding obligations in international law because its resolutions were not signed by any of the delegates.[11] And even if the document can be seen as a treaty, it was not binding on the Governments of South Vietnam or the United States, both of which refused to accept it.[12] Moreover, the Government of South Vietnam was not a party to the Cessation of Hostilities Agreement.

As French troops were withdrawn from Indo-China, the burdens placed on France by the Cessation Agreement should logically have fallen upon the South Vietnamese, but they refused to accept France's legal obligations. More seriously still, the South Vietnamese regime remained obdurate in refusing to hold free elections in Vietnam. It was backed publicly in this stance by the United States.[13] This frustrated and angered the North, which professed itself ready to honour its consultation and election commitments.

The Geneva Settlement, then, was largely ineffective for Vietnam. Possibly the most important point to emerge from it was that the participants clearly saw Vietnam as a single entity, rather than as two states. Differences existed as to which government was legitimate, but the conflict was seen essentially as a struggle between two potential governments for the control of one single country, despite the fact that one of the essential conditions of statehood, that the state in question should possess a government in effective control, was absent.[14] In reality, the North Vietnamese did have control over their zone, but the same could not be said of the Saigon Government in the South, which lacked control over Communist and even some non-Communist elements in that zone.

Thus the North Vietnamese sought to establish control over the whole territory, at first by means of the proposed elections, and later, when it became increasingly unlikely that these would take place, by supporting the National Liberation Front (NLF), with its military wing, the Viet Cong. The Americans, however, took the view that South Vietnam was a separate state, facing armed attack from the North. This was the basis of their claim to a right to intervene in collective self-defence.

The North Vietnamese position was less clear. One commentator has said that they 'wished to have the best of both worlds', by simultaneously characterising the war in the South as a 'civil war of national independence waged by the NLF against the Saigon regime which had been "created" and supported by the United States', while also claiming that the conflict was a struggle for national liberation by all the people of both zones of the country.[15]

It is beyond the scope of this study to attempt to decide which side was right, if either,[16] but brief consideration will be given to the question in a later chapter. It is proposed now to narrow the field and examine the background to New Zealand's intervention in the conflict.

2 New Zealand's Intervention

1. New Zealand's decision to intervene

It is now reasonably clear that the New Zealand Government's decision to participate in the Vietnam War, although accompanied by a good deal of rhetoric, was taken reluctantly. The military commitment was kept to a minimum, and despite the many idealistic words spoken in Parliament and elsewhere by members of the Government, the Prime Minister, Keith Holyoake, had made consistent efforts to encourage a peaceful solution. At the Commonwealth Prime Ministers' Conference in 1965 he advocated that the Viet Cong be included in any peace negotiations;[17] at a meeting of the ANZUS Council in June of the same year he 'strongly urged the initiation of peace moves';[18] and later in 1965 he is reported as saying that New Zealand was not opposing Communism as an ideology, but rather Communist aggression:

> If . . . the people of Vietnam freely choose communism . . . that would be their business.[19]

In spite of this conciliatory approach, on 16 June 1965 New Zealand notified the Security Council of its intention to enter the Vietnam War in a combat role.[20] This notification was made in compliance with the obligation under the Charter of the United Nations that any state taking measures in individual or collective self-defence shall immediately report such action to the Security Council.[21] Clearly, New Zealand was relying for the legality of its intervention in the war upon the notion of collective security. Indeed this was made explicit in the Government's note to the Soviet Ambassador which was circulated in the Security Council:

> The New Zealand Government has long been convinced of the need for international collective security and, contrary to the Soviet statement, its actions are firmly based on long standing adherence to the principles of international law, as embodied in the United Nations Charter.[22]

The note finishes with an interesting reflection of the attitude of Prime Minister Holyoake:

> The New Zealand Government has consistently maintained its support for a negotiated settlement in Viet Nam.[23]

The tenor of the Security Council document had been foreshadowed by a statement of the Prime Minister in the House of Representatives. On 10 May 1965, Dr Quat, the Prime Minister of the Republic of Vietnam (South Vietnam), sent a message to Prime Minister Holyoake asking New Zealand to commit combat troops in support of South Vietnam. On 27 May the Prime Minister announced to the House:

> In reaching its decision on this most important question the Government has borne in mind New Zealand's consistent record as a believer in collective security . . .[24]

He then gave notice of motion to the House on a resolution to support the Government's assistance to South Vietnam. The motion contained interesting wording. After having yet again 'reaffirmed' the country's belief in the principle of collective security, it added

> that the defence of the Republic of Vietnam cannot at the present time be carried out by the United Nations or any force drawn from a group of nations acceptable to the parties involved in the struggle . . .[25]

It also supported the search for a negotiated settlement in Vietnam. The wording is interesting for three reasons. First, although it mentions collective security, there is no express reference to SEATO. Yet New Zealand was to rely heavily on its SEATO commitments in later attempts to justify its involvement in the war. Secondly, it reflects a feeling that the United Nations was impotent, an attitude which was reinforced in debates in the House. And thirdly, the wording suggests that the Government was still inclined towards a negotiated settlement or a peacekeeping force of some kind in South

Vietnam rather than a full-scale conflict. That they must have realised that this was unlikely at that time is indicated by the words of the motion, and by the fact that New Zealand committed itself less than three months after Operation Rolling Thunder, inaugurating sustained American bombing of North Vietnam, was announced by President Johnson.[26] The inference is that New Zealand was only reluctantly joining the fray in a combat role. This reluctance will be dealt with later in this chapter.

On the same day, in his Speech from the Throne, the Governor-General mentioned the Vietnam War and subsequently spoke of SEATO and the doctrine of collective defence. But he made no express link between the conflict and the Treaty.[27]

On the following day, the Prime Minister spoke to his own motion.[28] He described the decision to assist the Republic of Vietnam as the most significant taken by any New Zealand government since the Korean War in 1950. He remarked that on his way home from the SEATO Conference in 1964 he went to Saigon and was asked by the Prime Minister for military assistance under the SEATO Treaty. This was granted in the form of non-combatant military engineers. He confirmed that New Zealand's first line of defence was in South-East Asia and that New Zealand had entered into treaties to that end,[29] and he made it plain that his Government did not regard the Vietnam War as a civil war or a popular uprising, but rather as 'ruthless communist aggression directed and supplied by Communist North Vietnam and openly encouraged, supported and partly supplied by Communist China'.[30]

The Prime Minister also addressed himself to the role of the United Nations, lamenting its inability to step in and deal with the problem. In a tacit reference to a dispute which had taken place in the General Assembly over the financing of United Nations peace-keeping forces,[31] he remarked that New Zealand was one of the few countries to have paid all its dues to the Organisation and that the country was committed to its success, but that, in the meantime

> the inescapable fact is that the only way we can bring about a settlement that will protect the people of South Vietnam is to join the collective de-

fence effort against this cruel, vicious, Communistic aggression until the Communists accept the need for a peaceful solution.[32]

This joining of the 'collective defence effort', he said, would be in accordance with New Zealand's treaty obligations:

> I have not time to go into detail, but only a few weeks ago members will have read that the SEATO Council, meeting in London, urged that member States should continue, and consistent with their commitments elsewhere, should increase their efforts in South Vietnam. Surely that is clear enough.[33]

This somewhat cursory comment appears to be intended to demonstrate that the New Zealand Government had consulted with other members of the Organisation, as required by the SEATO Treaty[34] in any situation in which the peace of the area is felt to be endangered. Such consultation would be inevitable in view of New Zealand's long-held position that South-East Asia is this country's first line of defence. Certainly there appears to be no suggestion that the SEATO Council could itself authorise armed intervention, a power which is not contained in the Treaty,[35] but which is reserved to each Member in accordance with its constitutional processes.

The Prime Minister also emphasised that the Government's decision was 'in accord with the Charter of the United Nations, which recognises the right of members to take collective action for self-defence.'[36]

If Mr Holyoake had set the scene for New Zealand's intervention in the war, it fell to his Deputy, Mr Marshall, aided by Mr Hanan, Attorney-General and Minister of Justice, to make the legal links express. Mr Marshall dealt first with the paralysis of the United Nations. He described the General Assembly as being 'tragically divided and hopelessly bankrupt',[37] and added that the Security Council was also powerless because any proposal to intervene in Vietnam would be met with a Soviet veto. He then stated that

> The Prime Minister has shown that the decision to send a combat unit to Vietnam is at the request of the Government of Vietnam and is in furtherance of our SEATO obligations. Members will see, if they read the

exchange of letters, that that is the basis of the request and of the response'.[38]

Mr Marshall remarked that 'it also happened' that artillery support was needed for the Australian infantry battalion, but if New Zealand failed to supply it, the Australians or the Americans would have done so.[39] This point will be considered later, when outside pressures on the New Zealand Government are examined.

Mr Marshall concluded by drawing the threads together: New Zealand could not 'shelter behind the United Nations . . . . The crux of the matter for us is that Communist aggression in Vietnam is a threat to us . . . . Our security and our way of life are at stake and we cannot stand aside'.[40]

It was left to Mr Hanan to explain the Government's interpretation of New Zealand's legal obligations under the SEATO Treaty. It is worth reproducing his words at some length, because the legality of New Zealand's position was thought by the Government to depend on this reasoning to a large extent:

> Under Article 4(1) of the Manila Treaty each member recognises that aggression by means of armed attack against any other member State or against a protocol State, such as the Republic of Vietnam, would endanger its own peace and security. We agree in that event to act to meet this danger in accordance with our constitutional processes. Under article 4(2) of the treaty, if these States are threatened in any other way the parties are to consult in order to agree on the measures which should be taken for the common defence. In the case of the protocol States we specifically tied any action under articles 4(1) and 4(2) to receiving a request or obtaining the consent of the Government concerned. It is not necessary, as is sometimes claimed, for any request to come through SEATO, nor is it necessary that such a request receive a unanimous response, for members have obligations which they should recognise and fulfil whether others do so or not. The attitude of SEATO was made clear at the SEATO Council meeting in London last month where it was agreed that member States should continue and, consistent with their commitments elsewhere, increase their assistance to South Vietnam. In terms of the Manila Treaty, all that is required for New Zealand to act in the event of aggression is that a request for assistance be received from the protocol

State concerned. Each Government is then free to act individually in accordance with its own constitutional processes. This action need not be taken jointly.

New Zealand's position is that it has received a request from a protocol State, the Republic of Vietnam. New Zealand has concluded that aggression is occurring, and that the independence of South Vietnam is threatened. The decision to provide assistance has been taken in accordance with our constitutional processes, that is, by Cabinet, which is responsible to Parliament, and is today answering to Parliament. In accordance with the Manila Treaty the members have been consulted on the measures to be taken, and the Government's action is undeniably in furtherance of its SEATO obligations under the Manila Treaty.[41]

These words show how the Attorney-General viewed New Zealand's legal position in the Vietnam War. Government speeches in this debate provide one or two interesting clues about other possible motives for involvement in the conflict. The first suggestion is found in Mr Hanan's own speech, shortly after his explanation of the legal position:

. . . the ultimate security of the peoples in this part of the South Pacific and in Australia and New Zealand lies only in the power, the support, and the goodwill of the United States . . . . Never was there a more obvious time for us to stand by the United States if we are to rely on the United States for support should we face aggression.[42]

And again, a little later:

. . . we are bound to defend our security and to support our friends, upon whom we depend for survival as an independent nation.[43]

These comments introduce an interesting political component, standing alongside the legal matters. The bulk of Mr Hanan's justification for New Zealand's involvement stresses SEATO obligations and the doctrine of collective defence. These later words, however, introduce a quite different element, that of the need to retain the goodwill of the United States, and as we shall see, that of Australia.

2. The American attitude to SEATO members

The picture painted by members of the New Zealand Government of their country's involvement in South Vietnam reveals one small nation coming to the aid of another, both in fulfilment of treaty obligations and on the premise that peace and security in the whole region was threatened by the attack on South Vietnam. Some concern that New Zealand should support the United States is also evident, but this is given no great prominence in the statements of Ministers in the House of Representatives. Indeed, Sir Leslie Munro, former diplomat and United Nations representative, explicitly disclaimed any American pressure:

> The United States has never asked us for active participation .... No pressure has ever been brought to bear upon us to intervene.[44]

The few available American documents which do examine New Zealand's role in the Vietnam War reveal, however, a somewhat different picture. As early as 1 May 1961 the Task Force for Vietnam, in a revised draft of its Report to the President, advised President Kennedy that the United States should

> obtain the political agreement [presumably from the SEATO membership] needed to permit the prompt implementation of SEATO contingency plans providing for military intervention in South Vietnam should this become necessary to prevent the loss of the country to communism. The United States should be prepared to intervene unilaterally in fulfilment of its commitment under Article IV, 2 of Manila Pact, and should make its determination to do so clear through appropriate public statements, diplomatic discussions, troop deployments, or other means.[45]

This advice is an early indication that the Americans were beginning to turn their eyes towards their allies, and it is buttressed by a report written by Vice-President Johnson after he returned from a visit to Saigon in May 1961. He had doubts about the potential effectiveness of SEATO and preferred a new alliance on a broader basis. He wrote:

> SEATO is not now and probably never will be the answer because of British and French unwillingness to support decisive action. Asian distrust of the British and French is outspoken. Success at Geneva will prolong SEATO's role. Failure at Geneva would terminate SEATO's

meaningfulness. In the latter event, we must be ready with a new approach to collective security in the area.

We should consider an alliance of all the free nations in the Pacific and Asia who are willing to join forces in defense of their freedom.[46]

When Johnson added that he envisaged such an organisation having a 'clear-cut command authority' it may be supposed that he felt such authority should be vested in the United States, as it had been in Korea.

On 10 October 1961 a paper called 'Concept of Intervention in Vietnam' appeared. It probably had its origins in the State Department and it seems to have reached at least Rusk and McNamara.[47] The paper purported to present a SEATO plan for Vietnam, but it explicitly assumed that 'planning would have to be on the basis of proceeding with whichever SEATO allies would participate'.[48] The paper also suggested, without offering any evaluation of them, some arguments for and against the plan. Included in the favourable arguments were the following points:

1. The effect on GVN [Government of Vietnam] morale of SEATO engagement in their struggle could be most heartening.
6. Introducing SEATO forces would give us for the first time some bargaining position with the Russians for a settlement in Vietnam.
7. If we go into South Vietnam now with SEATO, the costs would be much less than if we wait and go in later, or lose SVN [South Vietnam].[49]

The paper makes no reference to any South Vietnamese request for further help.

Another paper prepared at about this time for the National Security Council also discussed the role of SEATO.[50] It suggested that a SEATO commitment might turn out to be prolonged, which would enable the Communists to exploit weariness on the part of members participating in the conflict. Such members would look to the United States to solve the problem. If, on the other hand, SEATO intervention went well, Asian members would find renewed confidence in the Organisation and in the United States. Britain and France, however, were expected to oppose any SEATO action.

A personal memorandum from William Bundy, then Acting Secretary of Defence, written before 11 October 1961, and sent to McNamara, is also of considerable interest, the more so because Bundy was later to visit Australia and New Zealand. Bundy, apparently, saw an urgent need for support from the SEATO allies:

> Even if the decision at tomorrow's meeting is only preliminary — to explore with Diem and the British, Australians and New Zealanders would be my guess — it is clearly of the greatest possible importance. Above all, action must proceed fast.
> For what one man's feel is worth, mine . . . is that it is really now or never if we are to arrest the gains being made by the Viet Cong.[51]

The minutes of the National Security Council meeting with the President on 11 October were not available to the editors of the Pentagon Papers. But a memorandum written by one official records that it was agreed among other things that the State Department should push ahead with consultations with SEATO allies, principally the British and Australians, regarding SEATO actions in support of the deteriorating situation in Vietnam.[52]

The general United States attitude at this period in the war is well summed-up in a Memorandum for the President from Secretaries McNamara and Rusk. Dated 11 November 1961, in paragraph 7 the Memorandum records:

> From the political point of view, both domestic and international, it would seem important to involve forces from other nations alongside United States Category (B) forces in Vietnam. It should be difficult to explain to our own people why no effort has been made to invoke SEATO or why the United States undertook to carry this burden unilaterally. Our position would be greatly strengthened if the introduction of forces could be taken as a SEATO action, accompanied by units of other SEATO countries, with a full SEATO report to the United Nations of the purposes of the action itself.[53]

The Memorandum went on to recommend 'special diplomatic approaches' to SEATO, NATO and the OAS with the purpose of informing their members 'with selected members also informed individually'.[54]

That New Zealand was probably one of these 'selected members' is suggested by a Memorandum from the Joint Chiefs of Staff to the Secretary of Defence. Dated 13 January 1962, it was headed, 'The Strategic Importance of the South-East Asia Mainland'. After remarking that the United States had, as an unalterable objective, the prevention of the loss of South Vietnam and the remainder of the South-East Asian mainland to Communism, the Joint Chiefs of Staff asserted that if South Vietnam fell, Thailand would be the next target and SEATO would probably cease to exist. In paragraph 3.6, headed 'Possible Eventualities', the following statement appears:

> Of equal importance to the immediate losses are the eventualities which could follow the loss of the Southeast Asian mainland. All of the Indonesian archipelago could come under the domination and control of the USSR and would become a communist base posing a threat against Australia and New Zealand . . . .'[55]

This assertion was echoed by some New Zealand politicians as one justification for New Zealand's involvement in the war.[56]

It is clear from the above that American plans to involve New Zealand in the Vietnam War had their first formulation during the Kennedy Administration. Some approaches were apparently made, but it seems that the New Zealand Government played for time and that American pressure was, temporarily, not irresistible.

The war, in the meantime, carried on and intensified. The United States found itself less successful militarily than it had hoped and the Johnson Administration was attracting increasing criticism both at home and abroad for its conduct of the war. By 1964 the Americans felt keenly the need for support from their allies. At a meeting in the White House on 1 December 1964, President Johnson expressed the strong opinion that the United States needed 'new, dramatic, effective'[57] assistance from several countries. Australia, New Zealand, Canada and the Philippines were specifically mentioned, and a proposal to send a representative to the Governments of Australia, New Zealand and the Philippines was apparently approved. 'In each case, the representative was to explain our concept and proposed actions and request additional contributions by way of forces in the event the second phase of US actions were entered'.[58]

No time seems to have been wasted. On 4-5 December William Bundy held discussions in New Zealand and Australia. Other United States allies were also briefed. Australia and New Zealand were given full details of American plans to increase pressure on North Vietnam.[59] Both countries, contrary to the statement of Sir Leslie Munro,[60] were pressed to send troops to South Vietnam. New Zealand, however, was not prepared to make a commitment. The Government felt that the American policy decisions were probably necessary, but it doubted the wisdom of sending allied ground troops into South Vietnam, predicting that such a course of action would result only in a build-up of North Vietnamese troops in the South.[61]

New Zealand's reluctance to become involved in the war finally crumbled after the visit of Henry Cabot Lodge to Canberra in April 1965. The Australian response was prompt, and the Holyoake Cabinet now found itself politically embarrassed, although the New Zealand Government delayed for nearly another month. It has been pointed out that signature of the New Zealand-Australia Free Trade Area Agreement was imminent.[62] To have refused to follow Australia's lead might have offended not only the United States, but the Australians also, an undesirable situation because of New Zealand's balance of payments problems.

3. The Canberra viewpoint

If New Zealand was being nudged by the Americans into making a commitment in Vietnam, it seems that the country was being unequivocally shoved by the Australians. One Australian lawyer, Michael Sexton, has suggested that the Australian Government desired to enter South Vietnam at any price and actively pressed the United States to commit combat troops at every level of the conflict.[63] The Australians probably had two aims in pursuing this policy. First, American involvement in South Vietnam would, they thought, lock the United States firmly into South-East Asia, a situation which would be beneficial to Australian national security interests. Secondly, if Australia assisted the United States, then the

United States would feel obligated to return the favour should anyone threaten Australia. This analysis seems confirmed by a television interview in which the former Deputy Prime Minister, Sir John Marshall, commented:

> *Sir John:* 'Australia were then beginning to say privately to us, and more and more publicly, that this was something that they had to get committed to, particularly because they wanted to get the United States involved in South-East Asia as their main protection from a thrust from Communist China as it was then seen'.
> *Interviewer:* 'And loyalty meant we should be in there too?'
> *Sir John:* 'Yes, as part of that collective concept, because after all New Zealand can't do anything on its own. It has to rely on a collective security arrangement for its own defence'.[64]

Later in the same television programme Luke Hazlett, New Zealand High Commissioner in Canberra from 1964 to 1970, confirmed that the Australians were 'over-eager' at the start to involve both countries in Vietnam alongside the United States.[65]

By early January 1965, Australian diplomatic cables were clearly reflecting the desire of the Australian Government that the Americans should hit the communists harder.[66] Thus, at the very time when New Zealand was publicly discouraging escalation, Australia was actively promoting it with the United States, even though Bundy himself is on record as stating that, at this time, the Americans were not yet thinking in terms of ground forces.[67]

There was, however, an obstacle in the way of Australia's desired role in South Vietnam: the Government of that country had not asked for any assistance. Australia put pressure on the United States to secure such a request from Saigon, and eventually prevailed. It appears that New Zealand's refusal to act was a material factor in slowing down this approach to Saigon.[68] The long-awaited request for assistance was announced in Canberra on 29 April 1965. At six thirty that evening an urgent message was sent from Canberra to the Australian High Commissioner in Wellington instructing that the New Zealand government be informed that the Australian Prime Minister would announce, at eight o'clock, the commitment of an Australian battalion to Vietnam. Sexton comments:

It is likely that the New Zealanders were seriously offended by the lack of warning, especially as there was little chance of Australia's High Commissioner reaching the relevant New Zealand officials before 8 pm.[69]

4. Reluctant escalation

That New Zealand finally yielded to these pressures is history. It is of interest to note, though, that the United States remained aware of New Zealand's reluctance about its combat role in South Vietnam. In 1966 Bundy was succeeded as Special Assistant for National Security Affairs by Walt W. Rostow. On 11 May of the following year Rostow prepared a paper dealing with what he called a 'troop community chest operation for Vietnam'.[70] His paper included calculations showing that if each country involved in the war sent a proportion of its total armed forces equivalent to the commitment of the United States, the allied war effort would be augmented by 70,000 troops. Further, if each country contributed an increment to match an additional 100,000 American troops, then New Zealand's additional troop commitment would be approximately 400.[71] At this stage in the war the United States had committed about 14% of its armed forces to Vietnam. New Zealand's greatest troop strength in Vietnam was during 1968, when this country had some 548 personnel deployed there in different capacities. This represented just over 4% of New Zealand's total armed services' strength.[72] Thus, despite pressure brought to bear on allied heads of government by President Johnson in 1967, using Rostow's figures as a base line, New Zealand continued to react conservatively.

That the Americans anticipated that this would be the case is revealed in a memorandum sent to Rusk, McNamara, Rostow and Katzenbach on 13 July 1967. The memorandum, which emerged from a luncheon with President Johnson, was entitled 'Messages to Manila Nations and Possibilities for Additional Troop Contributions'. The memorandum showed the urgency and strength of American desire for greater commitment by allied countries. The President had ordered the writing of a series of letters making the need for additional forces clear and blunt. Even so, it was anticipated that New Zealand would make additional contributions that would only be modest in relation to the need perceived by the Americans.[73]

Finally, in 1968 the President asked his new Secretary of Defence, Clark Clifford, to oversee the preparation of a complete review of United States involvement in Vietnam.[74] The memorandum ultimately produced contained the following statement:

> A change in our bombing policy to include deliberate strikes on population centres and attacks on the agricultural population through the destruction of dikes would further alienate domestic and foreign sentiment and might well lose us the support of those European countries which now support our effort in Vietnam. It could cost us Australian and New Zealand participation in the fighting.[75]

It is apparent from this brief review of American attitudes to their SEATO allies that the United States was not at all prepared to sit back and wait for South Vietnam to request assistance under the Manila Treaty. It is also clear that American motives for trying to secure such assistance were not confined to the prosecution of policies of collective self-defence. Certainly the Americans made many statements emphasising this aspect of the allied contributions, but the working documents cited above show that other considerations were also at work, not the least of which must have been continuing Australian pressures. That these considerations were not openly acknowledged by the New Zealand Government is a matter of record.

It is now necessary to examine the nature of the SEATO alliance and to try to determine the legitimacy of its invocation as a reason for New Zealand's participation in the Vietnam War.

3 The Role of SEATO in Vietnam

1. The genesis of SEATO

In 1965, the New Zealand Government summed up the reasons for its involvement in Vietnam as follows:

> The Republic of Vietnam has looked to New Zealand along with other countries to provide the assistance that it needs. Under the Manila Treaty New Zealand has obligations with respect to the Republic of Vietnam. If we believe there has been aggression, then we have a firm duty to assist . . . Our action in South Vietnam is unquestionably taken in furtherance of our SEATO obligations; it is taken in concert with a number of SEATO allies; and it is taken in furtherance of a call of the SEATO Council.[76]

It is therefore important to examine the origins of New Zealand's adherence to the SEATO alliance.

The idea that New Zealand should participate in a defensive pact in South-East Asia was first raised seriously in Parliament in 1954. In words which were to prove too optimistic, the Minister of External Affairs, Mr Webb, explained to the House: ' . . . We in New Zealand . . . regard the formation of a South-East Asia alliance as a matter of extreme urgency . . . . The difficulty is not so much military aggression. That can be halted by military measures. Our problem is how to halt the insidious tactics of infiltration and subversion . . .'[77]

Two days later[78] Mr Webb elaborated by explaining that New Zealand was still uncertain about the exact form a South-East Asian alliance might take and who would belong to it:

> . . . at the moment the discussions are confined to Great Britain and the

United States. Later other countries like Australia and New Zealand will be brought into it, and I still hope that it will be possible to arrange a defensive alliance which I believe is essential for the security of this country . . . . It is not aimed at anyone in particular; it is just a defensive alliance. I was asked . . . whether a South-East Asian alliance implied support of intervention. Northing of the sort; it does not imply that. It is just intended to be a firm and unequivocal declaration that overt communist aggression would be resisted by the Allied Powers . . . [W]e will not by-pass the United Nations. It would be fatal if we did so. Any steps we take must be within the ambit of the Charter of the United Nations . . . [I]t would justify intervention just in the same way as we intervened in Korea where there was aggression. That was done under the auspices of the United Nations. That is the sort of thing we have in mind.[79]

A month later, the Minister of Defence was able to be more precise. He made it clear that allied endeavours were now directed towards setting up a South-East Asian Treaty Organisation along the lines of the North Atlantic Treaty Organisation.[80]

By 24 August, however, yet another direction seemed to be emerging. The Minister of External Affairs said that SEATO was not to be an offensive organisation but a defensive one. Defence was not necessarily military defence or only military defence. It could also, according to the Minister, be economic assistance, as under the Colombo Plan, enabling countries to build up their democratic institutions and raise the living standards of their people. This could be achieved by financial and technical assistance and that was what was meant by the term 'defence'.[81]

Events now moved apace, and on 8 September 1954, at the end of a conference held in Manila, the South-East Asia Collective Defence Treaty was signed. SEATO was born. On 30 September, the Minister of External Affairs, Mr Webb, rose in the House to make a statement on the SEATO agreement. He indicated that although it had been contemplated that the Ministerial part of the Conference would last a week, negotiations between London and Washington had enabled the conclusion of a treaty within three days.[82] After speaking briefly of Communist advances in South-East Asia the Minister stated that 'the principal object of the treaty is to give formal and public warning that the parties will stand together to resist any further acts of aggression'.[83]

This comment makes it clear that, as a result of British and American diplomatic manoeuvring, the prime concern of the Manila Conference was to set in place a military alliance designed to act as a backstop for the cease-fire negotiated in Geneva on 21 July. The Treaty does mention the wider 'defensive' aims expounded by Mr Webb on 24 August, but a reading of the document makes it clear that its main thrust was towards a military alliance by means of which it was hoped to deter further Communist advances in South-East Asia. It is now necessary, therefore, to examine the provisions of the Treaty and note the comments made by the Minister on certain individual Articles.

2. The SEATO Treaty and New Zealand's Approach

The foregoing sketch of the origins of the SEATO Treaty suggests that this was an alliance desired particularly by the United States for military purposes. Although Mr Webb's wider view of the purpose of the Treaty does receive some recognition in the document,[84] the following passage from the Pentagon Papers probably gives a fairly accurate picture of the American position:

> The failure [of the SEATO Treaty] was largely of American making. While Dulles wanted to put the communists on notice that aggression would be opposed, the Joint Chiefs of Staff insisted the United States must not be committed financially, militarily or economically to unilateral action in the Far East and that U.S. freedom of action must not be restricted. The two objectives conflicted and one cancelled out the other. Thus, Article IV of the treaty, the mechanism for collective action in case of enemy threat, did not pledge automatic response with force to force. Instead, each signatory promised to 'act to meet the common danger in accordance with its constitutional processes'. The United States, particularly Mr Dulles, tried to put teeth into SEATO through unilateral declarations of U.S. readiness to act. Dulles defined the obligations under Article IV as 'a clear and definite agreement on the part of the signatories, including the United States, to come to the aid of any member of the Pact who under the terms of this treaty is subjected to aggression'. However, Dulles

failed to instill the same dedication to instant intervention in the other SEATO members.[85]

This commentary reinforces the implication in Mr Webb's statement that the form of the Treaty was hammered out during internal and mutual discussions in the United States and Great Britain. The essential weakness of the SEATO Treaty is perhaps best illustrated by a comparison of the two key military articles in the NATO and SEATO Treaties respectively. Article 5 of the North Atlantic Treaty 1949 is quite specific:

> The Parties agree that an armed attack against one or more of them in Europe or North America shall be considered an attack against them all; and consequently they agree that if such an armed attack occurs, each of them, in exercise of the right of individual or collective self-defence, recognised by Article 51 of the Charter of the United Nations, will assist the Party or Parties so attacked by taking forthwith, individually and in concert with the other Parties, such action as it deems necessary, including the use of armed force, to restore and maintain the security of the North Atlantic area . . . .

The strength of the language in this Article caused concern in the United States Congress, because it was interpreted in some quarters as automatically committing the United States to go to war if a NATO partner were attacked. Both the Senate Committee and the Secretary of State reported on this Article. Both said that such an interpretation would be quite incorrect, and that such an automatic commitment would, moreover, be unconstitutional.[86]

Partly to avoid a recurrence of this problem, Article IV(1) of the SEATO Treaty was drafted in looser terms, borrowing language from Article 43(3) of the United Nations Charter.[87] The Article reads:

> Each party recognises that aggression by means of armed attack in the treaty area against any of the parties or against any state or territory which the parties by unanimous agreement may hereafter designate, would endanger its own peace and safety, and agrees that it will in that event act to meet the common danger in accordance with its constitutional processes . . . .

It has been suggested that Article IV(1) requires unanimous agreement before military action may be taken, but the wording of the paragraph does not support this interpretation. Unanimity clearly is required for the designation of territories, but the responsibility for taking action seems to be both several and joint.[88] That this was the view of the New Zealand Government, at least by 1965, is borne out by Mr Hanan's statement in the House already cited above.[89] It follows that '... in the absence of a collective decision by the parties as to the measures required, assistance in some form other than armed force would satisfy the duty to "act" stated in Article IV(1)'.[90]

New Zealand's view was that Article IV lay at the heart of the Treaty. In the House the Minister of External Affairs made some revealing remarks about the force and nature of the Article:

> Some people have said there is not very much binding about [it], but I would point out that no treaty can be made binding on any country. It is just a matter of a country being morally bound by its word. All that we can have in any treaty is an undertaking by each country involving a moral obligation....[91]

After thus striking at one of the fundamental norms of international law, that treaties are legally binding, Mr Webb continued:

> If honourable Members look at the ANZUS Treaty they will see that the wording, for all practical purposes, is the same,[92] and it is interesting to recall, as Mr Dulles reminded us, that it is practically the wording of the famous Monroe Doctrine of 1823.[93]

This is an interesting comparison, because there has long been a suspicion that the Monroe Doctrine existed essentially to serve the interests of the United States.[94] And despite the fact that several SEATO Members felt that the Treaty should cover all aggression, the Americans, by a protocol to the Treaty, expressly limited their obligations under Article IV(1) to cases of Communist aggression. The American justification for this, as understood by Mr Webb, was

> ... that out of the eight Powers the United States is the only one that has no territory in the area concerned, and the United States delegate em-

phasised that it would be straining the English language to say that any aggression in that area, other than Communist aggression, would endanger the peace and safety of the United States. But he did say that the United States recognised that Communist aggression anywhere, as well as in South East Asia, endangered the peace and safety of the United States.[95]

This view is tantamount to accepting that against Communist aggression the Monroe Doctrine is to be given global scope, which could not be justified in international law. It is sufficient to comment that, in effect, the United States was concluding a treaty somewhat different in substance from that adopted by the other SEATO Members, who chose not to limit the kind of aggression that was the subject of the Treaty and who had territorial interests in the Treaty area.

Article IV(2) of the SEATO Treaty deals with threats other than armed attack to the territory, sovereignty or political independence of any party. It includes 'any fact or situation which might endanger the peace of the area'. In such a case the parties are required to 'consult immediately in order to agree on the measures which should be taken for the common defence'.

Mr Webb refers to this type of situation as 'what we might call covert aggression as distinct from overt aggression',[96] and he remarks, with candour, 'it will be seen that there is *even less obligation* on the parties there than there is under paragraph (1)'[97] (emphasis added). This indication of the weakness of Article IV seems surprising in light of the great emphasis placed on it in 1965 to justify New Zealand's military commitment to the Vietnam War.

Article III of the Treaty is also interesting. In his comments of 24 August, Mr Webb expressed the view that 'defence' could include economic assistance, and this Article appears to enshrine that view. It states:

> The parties undertake to strengthen their free institutions and to co-operate with one another in the further development of economic measures, including technical assistance, designed both to promote economic progress and social well-being and to further individual and collective efforts of governments toward these ends.

The Minister's view on this aspect of the Treaty appears to have undergone a transformation during the Conference, because on 30 September he made the following comment:

> There is no intention at present to use SEATO as the medium through which this economic and technical assistance will be provided.[98]

This comment recalls the reticence of the American Joint Chiefs of Staff to restrict the United States' freedom of action by means of this Treaty and again suggests American influence in the final shape of the agreement.

As is almost universal with post-Second World War defence pacts, the SEATO Treaty emphasised the primacy of the United Nations in world peacekeeping. Article IV(1) lays down that measures taken under that paragraph 'shall be immediately reported to the Security Council of the United Nations'. The Preamble and Article I reinforce and reaffirm the fundamental provisions of the United Nations Charter, and Article VI states:

> This Treaty does not affect and shall not be interpreted as affecting in any way the rights and obligations of any of the parties under the Charter of the United Nations or the responsibility of the United Nations for the maintenance of international peace and security . . .

In the House Mr Webb emphasised the importance New Zealand attached to these provisions, and this attitude seems to have been consistently maintained by successive New Zealand Governments. In particular, during the Vietnam War, Mr Holyoake and other Ministers in his Cabinet expressed what appears to have been genuine regret that the peacekeeping machinery of the United Nations was unable to deal with the South-East Asian conflict. New Zealand's financial contributions to various peacekeeping operations were consistently maintained.[99]

Thus the impression one gains from statements made by New Zealand officials both before and after the SEATO Conference is of a diplomatic process dominated by American interests. The New Zealand Government's expectations about the outcome of the conference and the nature of SEATO appear to have undergone a number of changes. The idea that an eventual SEATO Treaty would resemble the North Atlantic Treaty proved to be mistaken. Instead, the document was compared with the Monroe Doctrine, which had its origins in American self-interest. What is more, the Treaty as signed by New Zealand and the other parties differed in one important respect from that signed by the United States. New Zealand, while clearly having Communist advances in mind, did not wish to restrict the Treaty's scope to this threat alone. The Americans, however, openly justified their position on the more tenuous ground of distinguishing between Communist aggression and other aggression in relation to their right to claim an interest sufficient to permit intervention under international law. Finally, New Zealand's hopes for a broader treaty involving economic and technical aid were only partially realised. While paying lip-service to these principles, the Treaty enshrined them only in a generalised form, and the New Zealand delegation returned home contemplating fulfilment of these pledges through agencies other than SEATO.[100]

The foregoing has outlined the genesis of the SEATO Treaty and New Zealand's attitude to it, and has contrasted this with the United States' viewpoint. It is now necessary to turn to the broader sphere of the international law of collective self-defence and to attempt to relate New Zealand's intervention in the Vietnam War, under the auspices of SEATO, to this body of law.

4 Collective Self-Defence in International Law

It is clearly beyond the scope of the present study to attempt an exhaustive survey of the international law of collective self-defence. Rather, the approach will be to examine those areas of the law of self-defence which have direct relevance to the Vietnam War and to compare various views on this law. These views will then be related to the participation of New Zealand in the Vietnam War. The legality of the war from the North and South Vietnamese and American points of view will be dealt with only where this is necessary to shed light on the legality of New Zealand's position.[101]

1. The notion of collective self-defence

It is a characteristic of most legal systems that they contain, to a greater or lesser degree, a notion of self-help or self-defence. From a jurisprudential point of view, one would expect that as a legal system grows in sophistication, it will increasingly take out of the hands of individuals the right to react to a perceived wrong, and will replace this right with more formal systems of redress. In municipal legal systems this development is accomplished relatively easily. In most countries, the power of the state is very great compared with that of individuals. In the international arena, however, there are far fewer actors, and none of them is of negligible power. Because of the doctrine of sovereign equality, a state will not readily concede that another state has the right to apply sanctions to it. And therefore, in times of conflict, states will often resort to self-help in a way that would not be open to an individual in a municipal legal system.

Nevertheless, even in the relatively loose-knit international legal system, the right to self-help has been circumscribed. As one scholar has aptly expressed it, 'it is the responsibility of the international community as a whole to ensure that the plea of self-defence is not advanced as an excuse for the illegal use of force'.[102] The right of self-defence today is both enshrined in and limited by the United Nations Charter, but certain principles have existed in international law since long before the Charter's inception.

The most important of these principles were expressed in *The Caroline Case*.[103] During the Canadian Rebellion of 1837 preparations for subversive activity in Canada were made in the United States. The Americans tried to prevent this, but British forces crossed the border, seized a ship, the *Caroline*, fired her and sent her over the Niagara Falls. Two American citizens were killed. Out of correspondence between the American and British Governments, three criteria for self-defence emerged: first, there had to be a wrong against the state exercising the right; secondly, the need to act had to be overwhelming and instant; thirdly, the action had to be reasonable and not disproportionate. These criteria, save perhaps the second, persist to some extent in international law even today. Obviously, however, when this notion of individual self-defence is extended to collective self-defence, a problem arises in relation to the first criterion: how can a third state, which has not been directly wronged, be justified in acting on behalf of or in concert with the wronged state? One rationale offered in a leading treatise on international law explains:

> Such extension of the notion of self-defence is a proper expression of the ultimate identity of interest of the international community in the preservation of peace. It is also a practical recognition of the fact that . . . unless some right of collective self-defence is recognised the door is open for the piecemeal annihilation of victims of aggression by a State or States intent upon the domination of the world. In that sense collective self-defence is no more than rationally conceived individual self-defence.[104]

This argument has a superficial appeal, but it has been pointed out that this is not so much self-defence, as a collective action for maintaining peace and security. That is, it is collective *defence*, but not collective *self*-defence.[105]

Bowett has suggested three theories on the basis of the right of collective self-defence.[106] The first involves an analogy with private law, where, provided there is a 'proximate relationship' between victim and protector, one person may intervene to protect another from aggression by a third party. In these cases the attack on the victim must have the character of violating the protector's 'legally recognised interests in the security of the victim'.[107] In the international sphere, then, if the third state can show that its own rights have been violated by the attack on the victim, it has a right of collective self-defence.

Secondly, Bowett postulates a collective right based on the duty to maintain international peace and redress breaches of international law. But he himself points out that the existence of any such duty in international law is doubtful, and adds that to admit such an 'interest' in international peace and security would enable unlimited action under the guise of self-defence and would defeat rather than confirm the principle.[108]

Bowett's third theory involves 'the principle that States may exercise collectively what is undoubtedly their individual right'.[109] This principle requires each participant in a collective action to have an individual right of self-defence, and the existence of this individual right will be a question of fact. The attraction of this view is that it distinguishes between collective self-defence, and the mere imposition of sanctions aimed at redressing breaches of international law. Before collective self-defence can be pleaded, two conditions must be satisfied: 'that each participating state has an individual right of self-defence: [and that] there exists an agreement between the participating states to exercise their rights collectively'.[110] It has been remarked that state practice, however, does not support this theory. For example, under the NATO Treaty 'the parties agree that an armed attack against one or more of them . . . shall be considered an armed attack against them all,'[111] and this undertaking is not contingent upon a threat to the interests of the parties not attacked.[112] The wording of Article IV(1) of the SEATO Treaty, however, states that 'each party recognises that aggression by means of armed attack . . . against any of the parties . . . would endanger its own peace and safety . . .' . It is questionable whether this form of wording is suffient to conform to Bowett's theory, in that there may not be enough self-interest implicit in the Article to satisfy his first condition.

2. *State practice before the UN Charter*

Bowett asserts that state practice before the Charter of the United Nations provides evidence that certain states 'considered a "proximate relationship" to exist between themselves and certain other states so that an attack upon those other states would constitute a threat to their own security'.[113] The primary example is that of the Monroe Doctrine, under which the United States unilaterally declared that an attack on any part of their hemisphere would threaten their security and would justify action in individual self-defence. Between 1938 and 1940 this stand crystallised into a collective security agreement among the American States in general.[114]

Other countries have also claimed that their national security gives them a special interest in other parts of the world. For example, at the time of the General Treaty for the Renunciation of War, 1928,[115] the British Government informed the United States that:

> There are certain regions of the world the welfare and integrity of which constitute a special and vital interest for our peace and safety . . . . Their protection against attack is to the British Empire a measure of self-defence.[116]

But this claim has been criticised on the ground that it fails to specify any geographical region.[117]

The Japanese in 1934 also claimed a special interest because of their territorial proximity to China, although they did not specify a consequent right of self-defence. Bowett points out that both these claims have a doubtful legal basis and bear 'no real relation to the concept of collective self-defence', because this would require 'not only the existence of the individual right of self-defence, but also an arrangement, whether formal or ad hoc, by the States affected dirrectly or indirectly by an attack to exercise their rights of self-defence in concert'.[118]

These claims bring to mind at once the repeated assertions of successive New Zealand Governments that New Zealand has a special interest in the defence of South-East Asia. These claims, which were discussed in Chapter Two, were formalised in New Zealand's communication to the Security Council of 16 June 1965.

It would be premature to examine whether Bowett's criticism applies also to New Zealand, because the additional element of the United Nations Charter must be considered in this context. Certainly New Zealand was party to a formal arrangement within the region. The question that must be asked, then, is whether New Zealand had an interest in South-East Asian peace and security independent of the SEATO Treaty, or whether any such interest arose only by virtue of and in dependence on the Treaty. An attempt will be made to answer this question when the nature and position of regional organisations under the Charter are examined.

3. The United Nations Charter and collective self-defence

The Charter of the United Nations takes a strong position on the use of force to settle international disputes. Article 2(3) requires states to settle their international disputes by peaceful means and Article 2(4) states:

> All Members shall refrain in their international relations from the threat or use of force against the territorial integrity or political independence of any state, or in any other manner inconsistent with the Purposes of the United Nations.

This requirement has become the norm in international law proscribing resorts to arms, and, as far as Members are concerned, it is subject to only two major international exceptions. The first is that the Security Council may authorise the use of force in certain circumstances.[119] The second is that armed force may be used in self-defence. Article 51, in its material part, states:

> Nothing in the present Charter shall impair the inherent right of individual or collective self-defence if an armed attack occurs against a Member of the United Nations, until the Security Council has taken measures necessary to maintain international peace and security .... [120]

Taken in combination, these two Articles appear to mean that, unless the Security Council orders military action, the use of armed force at an international level by a Member of the United Nations is prohibited in all situations other than when a Member is a victim of armed aggression. This prohibition, on the face of it, admits no exceptions, so that it follows logically that if a non-Member of the United Nations is attacked, a Member would not be acting legally in coming to its aid. The non-Member, of course, is bound by neither Article[121], so that the state concerned would be fully justified under pre-existing international law in using force to defend itself. It is also entitled to request assistance from its allies. The problem is, that if the state requested is a Member, it would breach Article 2(4) by assisting another state which did not fall within the exception created by Article 51.

The Vietnam situation gives rise to exactly this problem. South Vietnam was not a Member of the United Nations. This fact could not impair its 'inherent right' to defend itself, but it did make it illegal, on this interpretation of the Charter, for New Zealand, a Member, to assist it,[122] because, under the Charter, New Zealand may legally resort to armed force only if authorised by the Security Council or in order to defend another Member state which has been attacked.

It has been suggested that Article 2(6) of the Charter is wide enough to extend Article 51 to non-Member states. Article 2(6) reads:

> The Organisation shall ensure that states which are not Members of the United Nations act in accordance with these Principles so far as may be necessary for the maintenance of international peace and security.

There are two problems with this suggestion, however. The first is that the words of Article 2(6) are somewhat general and probably establish only that the actions of non-Members are of concern to the United Nations. Such states should be guided rather than bound by the principles of Article 2.[123] The second problem is that the paragraph clearly places a duty on the Organisation to see that non-Members keep the peace. It is hard to see how this obligation could be extended to a Member state acting without the authorisation of a competent organ of the United Nations. The authority conferred by the paragraph is an unusual one in international law because it does not depend on the consent of the state affected. This type of authority, by its nature, will be sparingly used. Something of the kind was used in 1948 when the Security Council ordered an immediate cease-fire in Palestine. The order was directed to, *inter alia*, the Government of Israel, which was not a Member at that time. If such authority is the intended thrust of the paragraph, it seems unlikely that it could be extended to unilateral unauthorised action by a Member state, or even to action by a group of such states. This would fly in the face of the clear words of Article 2(4) and Article 51. Nevertheless, one writer[124] has remarked that a literal interpretation of Article 51 is not supported by actual state practice and that states do regard themselves as having a right of collective self-defence of non-Members. This must have been the view of the New Zealand Government, which consistently claimed that its actions in Vietnam conformed totally with its obligations under Article 51.

If a literal interpretation of Article 51 is adopted, a further difficulty arises with New Zealand's involvement in the Vietnam War. New Zealand purported to assist South Vietnam according to its obligations under the SEATO Treaty. If, however, it was illegal to assist a non-Member, the SEATO Treaty can have no weight, because Article 103 of the Charter states:

> In the event of a conflict between the obligations of the Members of the United Nations under the present Charter and their obligations under any other international agreement, their obligations under the present Charter shall prevail.

This requirement would mean that, if Article 51 did not authorise New Zealand's involvement in Vietnam, New Zealand would be breaching Article 2(4), even though it was acting under its SEATO obligations. This would amount to a conflict of the type mentioned in Article 103, and Article 2(4) would prevail. Again, it does not seem that the New Zealand Government ever contemplated this conflict of obligations, and, indeed, state practice in general appears decisively to have rejected the literal interpretation.

Assuming, then, that state practice may lend some support to the wider interpretation of Article 51, it is necessary to seek a meaning for the term 'collective self-defence'. Kelsen revealed the contradiction inherent in the expression when he pointed out that 'no legal norm can change the fact that an attack directed against one state only is not an attack directed against another state'.[125] He concluded that the term 'collective self-defence' is inaccurate, preferring 'collective defence'. A state, in his view, is not exactly defending *itself* when it comes to the aid of another state under attack. In the context of a defence treaty like NATO, where an attack against one party is deemed to be an attack against all parties, this distinction may be somewhat academic; but under the SEATO Treaty it has more meaning. Article IV(1) says that an attack against one party will 'endanger ... [the] peace and safety of the others'. Endangering the peace and safety is certainly less than an armed attack and may not fall within the ambit of Article 51.[126]

Bowett takes a slightly different view of the term 'collective self-defence'.[127] He submits that it means simply that countries may exercise collectively their individual rights of self-defence. This interpretation necessitates the conclusion that ' . . . it does not, therefore, generally extend the right of self-defence to any state which desires to associate itself in the defence of a state acting in self-defence'.[128] This interpretation would be inconsistent with the general prohibition under the Charter of the use of force and with the system of collective security under the supervision of the Security Council.

The problem with Bowett's view is that it means that, in order to justify its intervention, a third state must show that its own substantive interests have been affected, for it is only if this is so that the intervening state can be collectively exercising its individual right of self-defence. But this view simply does not accord with state practice and would, if adopted, lead to sophistic distortions of states' real motives for helping one another. For example, New Zealand may have a real and substantive interest in the security of Australia and perhaps a similar though less intense interest in that of Malaysia.

New Zealand's interest in both countries has historical, legal and institutional links because of common British influences. With Australia there is a clear military identity, and this may extend to Malaysia. But with Vietnam such links never existed. How remote does the chain of causation have to become before New Zealand's interest ceases to be sufficient? Bowett does not answer this question, and it is doubtful whether a firm answer is possible. It may be safer, therefore, to seek another basis in international law for actions of the kind undertaken by New Zealand in Vietnam. New Zealand was not attacked, and was therefore not defending itself, either individually or collectively. New Zealand did, however, join in the collective defence of South Vietnam, and it justified this most frequently by reference to the regional defence treaty concluded under SEATO.

4. Collective defence and regional arrangements

Kelsen has remarked that collective defence rights need not necessarily be formalised in an international treaty before aggression actually occurs.[129] Nevertheless, states have consistently felt a desire to formalise such defence treaties, and examples are numerous. Most such treaties are regional, being concluded by states sharing roughly the same geographical area. Collective defence under such treaties is usually justified by reference to Article 51 and to Chapter VIII of the Charter, which is headed 'Regional Arrangements'. Bowett remarks that there are two essential differences between collective defence under Article 51 and regional arrangements for security. First, collective defence may be undertaken without the prior authorisation of the Security Council, whereas enforcement action under regional arrangements must be authorised in advance.[130] Secondly, under Article 51, Members need only report to the Security Council 'measures taken . . . in the exercise of their right of self-defence', whereas under Article 54, states involved in regional arrangements have a duty that 'the Security Council shall at all times be kept fully informed of activities undertaken or in contemplation . . . '.

There is an important difference in scope between actions under

Article 51 and actions under Chapter VIII. Article 51 is confined to actions in self-defence, as has already been discussed. However, Article 52(1) states:

> Nothing in the present Charter precludes the existence of regional arrangements or agencies for dealing with such matters relating to the maintenance of international peace and security as are appropriate for regional action, provided that such arrangements or agencies and their activities are consistent with the Purposes and Principles of the United Nations.

This Article clearly contemplates action wider than simple self-defence. Bowett's substantive interest principle loses its relevance when it is contemplated that regional organisations may actually take enforcement action to maintain peace and security. The obligations will be different in each case. For an organisation like SEATO, it is necessary to ask whether its Members are involving themselves in a given conflict for reasons of self-defence, or in order to restore or maintain peace and security in the region. If action is for the second reason, a new fetter arises. Article 53 of the Charter says, in part:

> ... no enforcement action shall be taken under regional arrangements or by regional agencies without the authorisation of the Security Council ....

Bowett expresses it well when he writes:

> If the juridical concept of self-defence is to have any meaning it must ... be distinguished from collective action for the purpose of maintaining international peace and security within a defined region. The latter we would characterise as collective security action.[131]

Such collective security action really amounts to the utilisation of powers delegated by the Security Council. If the Security Council is unable to act because of the veto of one or more of the Permanent Members, residual responsibility lies in the General Assembly.[132] If the General Assembly also fails to act, to say that a further residual authority lies in regional groups to act on their own initiative would be extremely suspect, and would amount to legitimising a breakdown of the fundamental principles of the Charter.

In the Vietnam War, collective action by SEATO as such was never authorised by either the Security Council or the General Assembly,[133] nor did they authorise collective action by the individual Member states of SEATO. Thus intervention in the Vietnam War by states Members of both SEATO and the United Nations, including New Zealand, must be based in law, if at all, on Article 51, not Chapter VIII.

It is therefore necessary to consider the relationship between regional defence treaties and the Charter, and in particular whether action under such treaties conforms with Article 51. The discussion will assume the wider interpretation of Article 51, because to do otherwise would preclude any examination of the Vietnam War for the reasons given earlier in this Chapter.

The most important question is whether action under treaties such as NATO, SEATO and ANZUS can be correctly characterised as self-defence, especially if Bowett's view is accepted that self-defence is available only to a state defending its substantive rights. As has been noted earlier in this study, it is questionable whether, as a juridical concept, a treaty can, by the mere fact of its existence, bring mutual assistance within the ambit of legitimate self-defence. It is probable that there must be some factor other than the treaty alone which will endow a state with an interest sufficient to permit recourse to arms. If this is true as among Member states of the United Nations, it must be so *a fortiori* when the state being assisted is a non-Member. Geographical proximity is an obvious example of such a factor. Any armed attack on Australia or New Zealand would be of primary concern to the other country on this basis alone. But other kinds of interdependence might suffice. For example, economic and strategic considerations reinforce the American claim that the United States has a special interest in the Middle East. As Bowett puts it:

> The difficulty is . . . to distinguish real interdependence which can alone afford a legal basis for the right of self-defence from a mere claim to 'spheres of interest', which ranks as a political rather than a legal doctrine.[134]

In the South-East Asian context, the United States' reservations to the SEATO Treaty, mentioned above, provide an interesting example of a tacit acknowledgment of this distinction. The Americans, it will be recalled, limited their interest in the region to cases of Communist aggression. This was explained to the New Zealand House of Representatives as being because, alone among the SEATO Members, the United States had no territory in the region.[135] This is tantamount to acknowledging that there is no geographical nexus between the United States and South-East Asia. The corollary of this point is that the other SEATO Members, who did not limit themselves to opposing only Communist aggression, felt that they had a sufficient geographical proximity to potential trouble spots in South-East Asia to justify a collective defence pact. It should be remembered that the SEATO Treaty was concluded less than a decade after the defeat in the Second World War of Japan, which had adopted an 'island-hopping' strategy through South-East Asia and the Pacific. It was also the period of the cold war between the Communist bloc and the West, when Sino-Soviet policies of Communist world domination were being taken seriously. Members of the New Zealand Government of the day frequently said that the South-East Asian region had more to fear from covert aggression, an ideological battle to win the poorer countries for Communism, than from armed attack.[136] This fear was based on the 'domino theory', which the New Zealand Minister of External Affairs put into the following words in the House:

> Anyone who glances at the map will see there is a continuous slice of territory, comprising China, Indo-China, Thailand, Burma, and Malaya. Then the narrow strait of Malacca separates Malaya from the islands of Indonesia, and those islands look like so many stepping stones leading down to Australia and New Zealand.[137]

It will also be recalled that New Zealand was emphatic about the need for assistance to the South-East Asian countries, believing technical and economic help to be the best insurance against Communist domination, and was disappointed when this was not made a cornerstone of the SEATO Treaty.

It appears, then, that New Zealand did have genuine concerns about the future of the South-East Asian region and that these concerns pre-dated the SEATO Treaty. New Zealand had already made a commitment to the region under the Colombo Plan, and later assisted South Vietnam in a non-military manner. Whether sufficient interdependence exists will, in the final analysis, be a question of fact to be determined by an examination of the practices of the state claiming the nexus. It appears that New Zealand was acting in good faith when it claimed a real legal interest in South-East Asia, as opposed to a political conviction that this was a sphere of interest. It can probably be stated with safety, therefore, that the SEATO Treaty did not, by itself, create this legal interest, but rather reflected and formalised it, as far as New Zealand was concerned.

Hence it probably makes little difference in legal terms whether New Zealand undertook military aid to South Vietnam under the auspices of the SEATO Treaty or independently of it. It has been doubted whether collective self-defence under Article 51 requires a pre-existing treaty of assistance,[138] but because New Zealand consistently justified its intervention in the Vietnam War in terms of its SEATO obligations, it is necessary now to examine the legal nature of those obligations.

5. SEATO and the duty to defend

It has been argued that intervention in Vietnam under the SEATO Treaty was illegal on two counts: first, because the Treaty requires the unanimity of all signatories before military action may be undertaken, and such unanimity was absent; and secondly, because even with unanimity, action by a regional organisation must be authorised in advance by the Security Council under Article 53, and no such authorisation was granted. Both these arguments are fallacious, however.

American Secretary of State Rusk made the following observation on the supposed requirement of unanimity:

> The language of this treaty is worth careful attention. The obligation it imposes is not only joint but several. The finding that an armed attack has occurred does not have to be made by a collective determination before the obligation of each member becomes operative. Nor does the treaty

require a collective decision on actions to be taken to meet the common danger. If the United States determines that an armed attack has occurred against any nation to whom the protection of the treaty applies, then it is obligated to 'act to meet the common danger' without regard to the views or actions of any other treaty member.[139]

A similar view was expressed by the New Zealand Minister of Justice:

> It is not necessary, as is sometimes claimed, for any request to come through SEATO, nor is it necessary that such a request receive a unanimous response, for members have obligations which they should recognise and fulfil whether others do so or not.[140]

Thus, in the light of this interpretation, each party must decide for itself whether an 'armed attack' has occurred, and what action it will take to meet the common danger. The wording of Article IV(1) supports this approach: unanimous agreement is required only in the context of designating territories, not for the taking of measures. For this latter purpose the Treaty simply requires the parties to 'consult immediately in order to agree on the measures which *should* be taken for the common defence' (emphasis added). The absence of an imperative in this sentence arguably indicates severed responsibility. As well, the SEATO Council has no specific powers except to provide for consultation.[141] Thus a military response to a request for aid under Article IV(1) is not mandatory, and unanimity is not required.

The second objection, concerning prior authorisation by the Security Council, can be dealt with equally shortly. First,

> . . . it is clear that the parties to a regional arrangement are entitled to combine together in measures of collective self-defence without the prior authorisation of the [Security] Council . . .; the right of collective self-defence is governed by Article 51 and is entirely independent of the provisions regarding regional arrangements.[142]

Secondly, such actions in no way prejudice the Security Council's power to act, because the Charter prevails over regional treaties. And thirdly, it is arguable that, notwithstanding the emphasis placed by Vietnam participants on the SEATO Treaty, the actions of those states participating in the war were in reality legally outside the

SEATO framework. Because SEATO imposed no mandatory military response and because the SEATO Council had no real powers, it is at least possible that the states undertaking a combat role in Vietnam were doing so under Article 51 of the Charter, regardless of the SEATO Treaty.[143] In other words, all that was required for the presence of the troops of SEATO Members in South Vietnam was that country's agreement. If that were not enough, it is hard to see how the SEATO Treaty could fill the gap.

5 The Vietnam War: Civil or International?

It has been stated by some critics of allied involvement in the Vietnam War that South Vietnam was not a separate, independent state. Rather, North and South Vietnam were, under the 1954 Geneva Accords, a single entity, so that the war between the rival Governments was in reality a civil war, although differing in some respects from a 'classic' civil war.[144] However, this may be to confuse the idea of a single state with a single people. Certainly there is nothing novel about a single people forming more than one state. The independent Arab States are a good example.[145]

It has already been shown that an assumption of the independent statehood of South Vietnam was fundamental to New Zealand's decision to enter the conflict. But even if South Vietnam is not thought to have had all the characteristics of independent statehood, it does not follow inevitably that New Zealand's involvement amounted to an illegal intervention in a civil war.

By the time it became apparent that the Geneva cease-fire line, which had been intended to be only a provisional demarcation, would become permanent, the Government in the North had already made good its control over all the territory allotted to it. The Government in the South, however, never succeeded in doing the same. Yet both groups claimed to be the Government of the whole country.

North Vietnam had two basic arguments, which were not wholly compatible. First, they claimed that the Vietnamese were one people and that Hanoi was their true Government. But secondly, they also argued that the National Liberation Front was the true Government of South Vietnam, thereby implying that this latter was a separate state.

The United States and New Zealand agreed with the second conclusion, but did not accept the NLF, claiming instead that South Vietnam was an independent state subject to external armed aggression.[146]

Greig remarks that the general tendency among writers has been to regard North and South Vietnam as separate *de facto* states, but says that this is a dangerous concept. It is one thing to talk about governments as *de facto* or *de jure;* it is another to treat states in this way:

> A state has a certain status under international law, and that is *ex hypothesi de jure*. The nearest to *de facto* recognition of an entity approximating to a state is recognition of the government as *de facto* exercising authority in a particular area . . . . On the international plane *de facto* recognition has evidentiary value in relation to the area and extent of the control exercised by the entity concerned, but it cannot constitute it a state.[147]

The Americans claimed as evidence of South Vietnam's statehood the fact that it had been admitted to membership of several specialised agencies of the United Nations.[148] But this claim is dubious, because full statehood has frequently not been required for such admission.

But even if South Vietnam were not a full state, New Zealand's involvement, as already noted, does not necessarily amount to illegal intervention in a civil war. As the Americans pointed out, hostilities across a cease-fire line need not be excluded as a legitimate reason for actions in collective self-defence:

> . . . there is no warrant for the suggestion that one zone of a temporarily divided state . . . can be legally overrun by armed forces from the other zone, crossing the internationally recognised line of demarcation between the two. Any such doctrine would subvert the international agreement establishing the line of demarcation, and would pose grave dangers to international peace.[149]

This proposition seems to have support among the writers:

[Although this] seems on its face to be civil strife, if such lines have long been continued and widely recognised, as have those in Germany, Palestine, Kashmir, Korea, Viet Nam and the Straits of Formosa, they assume the character of international boundaries. Hostilities across them immediately constitute breaches of *international* peace, and justify 'collective defence' measures.[150]

Thus the Vietnam War seems to have been a hybrid between a civil war and a war across international boundaries. State practice in international law has not evolved to a point where it is possible to say with any degree of certainty what rules apply to such a situation. The North Vietnamese appear to have recognised, at least by implication, the mixed nature of the conflict. The SEATO allies, on the other hand, preferred to justify their involvement in the traditional terms proper to an international conflict. As already noted, a great deal of scholarly analysis of this question has taken place and all that the present study can do is to direct a reader to some of this material by means of the footnotes to this work.[151] Nevertheless, it is hoped that this brief survey of the problems will provide a useful starting point and a sufficient background to put the main concerns of the present study in their wider context, and to prepare the ground for the conclusions that follow.

6

Conclusions

It should now be possible to draw the threads together and attempt to reach some conclusions about the legality or otherwise of New Zealand's participation in the Vietnam War.

As we saw in the previous Chapter, different sets of considerations arise depending on whether the Vietnam War is classified as international or civil. This study has concentrated on the international nature of the war for three main reasons. First, most writers seem to concur in the opinion that the Vietnamese conflict was not *simply* a civil war, some holding that it was purely international, others arguing that it was a hybrid of the two. Secondly, New Zealand's participation was unequivocally predicated on a conviction that the conflict was international, so that to treat it as a civil war would preclude an examination of New Zealand's justification for its involvement. And thirdly, if the war is regarded as civil, it must be seen as a special type of civil war, and it is not at all certain that state practice has evolved a set of rules adequate for such circumstances.[152]

What is important for the purposes of this study is to ask whether the New Zealand Government made its determination about the international nature of the war in good faith.

Indeed the requirement of good faith is important in this context for another reason. It is high among the 'general principles of law recognised by civilised nations' which constitute one of the sources of international law.[153] Hence, New Zealand's good faith may be questioned. For New Zealand to invoke the rights conferred upon it by the Charter and by the SEATO Treaty, it must have determined that an international armed attack against an ally was taking place, and that its own peace and safety were threatened.[154] As has been shown in Chapters Two and Three, many official statements indicate that this was the Government's view. However, examination of American materials also revealed that, notwithstanding some protestations to the contrary, New Zealand's decision to intervene was almost certainly conditioned by persistent and weighty pressure from the United States and Australia. This pressure makes it legitimate to raise the question of good faith. Taken alone, pressure from allies who were not under attack would probably not be enough to justify intervention under the banner of collective self-defence. That is, if New Zealand's only reason for entering the war was that it should stand alongside the United States, in return for past and future favours, this could amount to something less than good faith and might render such participation suspect. On balance, however, the sources examined indicate that, while this obligation may have been one reason for New Zealand's involvement, it was neither the only nor even the principal reason. Thus a serious breach of good faith can probably be discounted. The question of good faith is one of fact, not law, in this instance.

The next question is whether New Zealand had a general right of collective self-defence in relation to South Vietnam. Of Bowett's three theories about the basis of such a right, only that dealing with a 'proximate relationship' between the victim and the protector has any application to Vietnam. That New Zealand claimed such a relationship with South-East Asia, including South Vietnam, has been made clear; but the question of how remote such a relationship must become before there is insufficient proximity was also raised. We have seen that a variety of links, such as geography, strategic importance or economics, could satisfy the requirement, but that these are more restricted in the case of self-defence than they are when regional enforcement action is taken under Chapter VIII of the Charter. Because the conditions for such regional action were not met in the Vietnam War, it remains to ask whether New Zealand's claim to a proximate relationship with South Vietnam can be sustained. If Bowett's suggested principle is to be applied strictly, New Zealand may have been hard put to establish 'legally recognised interests' in the security of South Vietnam. But we have already seen in earlier Chapters that New Zealand did regard itself as having such an interest and that in the political context of the times, this was probably genuine.

If, however, New Zealand is thought not to have had such a legally recognised interest, some other legal basis must be sought to justify New Zealand's role in the war. If this basis is thought to lie in Article 51 of the Charter, it will depend first and foremost on whether the Article is given the literal or the wider interpretation referred to above. If the literal interpretation is followed it seems inescapable that New Zealand did not enjoy the right of collective self-defence of South Vietnam, a non-Member of the United Nations, because of the operation of Article 2(4) of the Charter in combination with Article 103. On this interpretation New Zealand's combat role in Vietnam must have been illegal.

But if we adopt, as state practice suggests we must, the wider interpretation of Article 51, New Zealand's actions were *prima facie* legal unless some negative factor or factors can be isolated.

According to the technical requirements of Article 51, New Zealand appears to have fulfilled all its obligations. It notified the Security Council promptly of its intention to act and it consistently expressed its willingness to abide by the provisions of the Charter and to accept any Security Council decisions made with reference to the Vietnam War.

Another negative factor could be any presence of New Zealand troops north of the Seventeenth Parallel, because, if New Zealand's view that South and North Vietnam were separate states is accepted, this presence could amount to an incursion by New Zealand forces into the territory of a non-consenting state. In the event it is not necessary to examine the possible justification as self-defence of any such incursion, because official statements from the New Zealand Ministry of Defence indicate that 'throughout the time of this commitment [no New Zealand forces], as a matter of policy, operated outside the territory of South Vietnam. Certainly none saw service above the Seventeenth Parallel.'[155] Thus a qualitative as well as a quantitative difference can be seen between New Zealand and

American involvement in the war. Whereas many American actions in Vietnam arguably cannot be brought within the scope of Article 51,[156] it does seem that New Zealand was not in breach of its provisions. It thus remains only to assess the effect, if any, of the SEATO Treaty on New Zealand's involvement in the war.

It has been pointed out that, by itself, the SEATO Treaty would probably not have been enough to justify involvement in Vietnam if taken as creating New Zealand's only interest in that territory. Likewise, it is doubtful whether the mere presence of New Zealand troops there, under the auspices of the Treaty, would have been sufficient to create an interest. Any attack on the troops would have been incidental to the attack on the Government of South Vietnam and would thus not have created, *per se*, an interest.

Further, it has been observed that Article IV of the Treaty does not make mandatory a military response to aggression against a state protected by the Treaty. Other types of assistance would suffice, and even no action at all would not be in breach of the letter, as opposed to the spirit, of the Treaty.

New Zealand did, however, eventually take military action, as it was entitled, but not obliged, to under the Treaty. The arguments about unanimity and prior United Nations authorisation have already been dealt with. It therefore seems that New Zealand's intervention under SEATO could have been illegal only if it incidentally breached a provision of the United Nations Charter, because in the event of any conflict of obligations the Charter prevails. That no such breach did occur emerges from the discussion in Chapter Four. Indeed, it is arguable that if New Zealand could justify intervention under Article 51, it was not strictly necessary ever to invoke the SEATO Treaty. New Zealand did choose to invoke it, however, in response to a request under Article IV(3) from South Vietnam. Therefore the only possible ground for attacking New Zealand's involvement under SEATO would be on the question of good faith.

On this point we have seen that American and Australian influence was far from negligible, both at the time of SEATO's inception and later when certain of its Members became involved in the Vietnam War. There is certainly enough evidence to suggest that New

Zealand's invocation of the SEATO Treaty to justify the sending of combat troops to South Vietnam was somewhat disingenuous,[157] even though formal procedures appear to have been complied with.

It may well be, therefore, that New Zealand's reliance on SEATO was not totally in good faith. However the same probably cannot be said of New Zealand's actions under Article 51, and it is not clear that, in legal terms, New Zealand ever actually needed to invoke SEATO to justify entering the Vietnam War. That is, if intervention could be justified under Article 51, SEATO was not needed, and if intervention could not be justified under Article 51, SEATO could make no difference.

Thus, New Zealand's reliance on the Treaty was a matter of politics rather than of law, and subject to the provisos earlier explained about the nature of Article 51 and the international character of the war, New Zealand's intervention was probably legal.

This conclusion may surprise, and even anger, critics of New Zealand's role in the war. It should be pointed out, however, that the legality and the morality of an action can quite often be separate issues. Many scholars feel that the United States acted both immorally and sometimes illegally in Vietnam. That New Zealand may have acted legally does not mean that it acted morally. The relationship between morals and the law is a difficult jurisprudential question at any time, and never more than when it is interwoven with international politics. Those who condemn New Zealand for its role in the war on moral grounds, should nevertheless be grateful that illegality was not added to immorality.[158]

Abbreviations

AJHR	Appendix to the *Journals of the House of Representatives*
AJIL	*American Journal of International Law*
ASIL	*American Society of International Law*
BFSP	*British Foreign and State Papers*
BYBIL	*British Yearbook of International Law*
Harv. LR	*Harvard Law Review*
ICJ Reports	*Reports of the International Court of Justice*
LNTS	*League of Nations Treaty Series*
NZPD	*New Zealand Parliamentary Debates*
OLR	*Otago Law Review*
UKTS	*United Kingdom Treaty Series*

Notes

1. Document S/6435.
2. Document S/6449.
3. Agreement between the Commander-in-Chief of the French Union Forces in Indo-China and the Commander-in-Chief of the People's Army of Viet-nam on the Cessation of Hostilities in Viet-Nam, Article 1.
4. Ibid., Article 1.
5. Ibid., Article 14(a): 'Pending the general elections which will bring about the unification of Viet Nam, the conduct of civil administration in each regrouping zone shall be in the hands of the party whose forces are to be regrouped there in virtue of the present agreement.'
6. Ibid., Article 16.
7. See Articles 17 and 18.
8. Article 19: 'With effect from the date of entry into force of the present Agreement, no military base under the control of a foreign state may be established in the regrouping zone of either party; the two parties shall ensure that the zones assigned to them do not adhere to any military alliance and are not used for the resumption of hostilities or to further an aggressive policy.'
9. See Chapter VI of the Agreement.
10. Final Declaration of the Geneva Conference on the Problem of Restoring Peace in Indo-China, paragraph 7.
11. See, for example, Quincy Wright, 'Legal Aspects of the Viet-Nam Situation' 60 AJIL 750 (1966); also D.W. Greig, *International Law* 2nd ed. 906; also Akehurst (1973-76), 3 OLR, 39, at 40-2. That the Final Declaration was not binding was also the view taken by the Government of the United Kingdom, which stated that it 'was not a formal instrument in the usual treaty form. It was not signed and appears to have the character properly of a statement of intention or policy on the part of those member States of the Conference who approved it'. HMSO Misc. No. 25 (1965), Cmnd. 2834, p. 16, para 41.

12. Ibid. See also the Memorandum on the Legality of United States Participation in the Defense of Viet-Nam, March 4, 1966, III D; also Akehurst loc. cit., n.11, supra.
13. See Legality Memorandum, loc.cit., n. 12, supra. The United States took the view that South Vietnam was not bound, but even if it had been bound, 'the conditions in North Vietnam during that period were such as to make impossible any free and meaningful expression of popular will'.
14. See the Montevideo Convention on the Rights and Duties of States 1933, Article 1(c).
15. See Greig, loc.cit., n.11 supra, p. 909.
16. For a comprehensive collection of writings on the Vietnam War see the three-volume collection *The Vietnam War and International Law,* sponsored by the American Society of International Law, ed. Richard A. Falk.
17. See W.K. Jackson, 'New Zealand and Southeast Asia' *Journal of Commonwealth Political Studies,* Vol. 9, No. 1, p. 8.
18. Ibid.
19. External Affairs Review, December 1965, p. 16, quoted in Jackson loc.cit.
20. Document S/6449.
21. UN Charter, Article 51.
22. Document S/6449.
23. Ibid.
24. (1965) 342 NZPD 1.
25. Ibid., p. 2.
26. Operation Rolling Thunder was announced on 28 Febraury 1965. It was to be a limited continuous air campaign against the North, intended to bring about a negotiated settlement on terms favourable to South Vietnam.
27. (1965) 342 NZPD 3.
28. Ibid., pp. 7ff.
29. Ibid., p. 8.
30. Ibid., pp. 8 and 9.
31. *Certain Expenses of the United Nations* case, ICJ Reports 1962, 151. The case concerned an advisory opinion which the General Assembly sought from the ICJ concerning the refusal of France and Soviet bloc members to pay their share of the costs of the UNEF and ONUC peacekeeping forces on the grounds that both were unconstitutional. The Court, by a majority of 9 to 5 found that they were not, but the states concerned still refused to pay. The matter has never been satisfactorily resolved.
32. (1965) 342 NZPD 10.

33. Ibid.
34. SEATO Treaty, Article IV (2) provides: 'If, in the opinion of any of the parties, the inviolability or the integrity of the territory or the sovereignty or political independence of any party in the treaty area or of any other State or territory to which the provisions of paragraph 1 of this article from time to time apply is threatened in any way other than by armed attack, or is affected or threatened by any fact or situation which might endanger the peace of the area, the Parties shall consult immediately in order to agree on the measures which should be taken for the common defence.'
35. See SEATO Treaty, esp. Art. IV (1).
36. (1965) 342 NZPD 10. And see UN Charter, Art. 51.
37. (1965) 342 NZPD 16.
38. Ibid.
39. Ibid., p. 17.
40. Ibid.
41. Ibid., p. 21.
42. Ibid., p. 22.
43. Ibid., p. 24.
44. Ibid., p. 53.
45. *The Pentagon Papers,* Senator Gravel edition, Vol. 2, p. 42.
46. Ibid., Vol. 2, p. 58.
47. See Ibid., Vol. 2, pp. 74-5.
48. Ibid., Vol. 2, p. 76.
49. Ibid., Vol. 2, p. 76.
50. Ibid., Vol. 2, pp. 77-8.
51. Ibid. Vol. 2, p. 79.
52. Ibid., Vol. 2. p. 80.
53. Ibid., Vol. 2. p. 113.
54. Ibid., Vol. 2, p. 116.
55. Ibid., Vol. 2, pp. 662-3.
56. For example, Deputy Prime Minister Marshall. See infra, p. 17
57. *The Pentagon Papers,* Senator Gravel edition, Vol. 3, p. 249.
58. Ibid., Vol. 3, p. 250.
59. Other governments were told less. Ibid., Vol. 3, p. 257.
60. See infra, p. 21
61. *The Pentagon Papers,* Senator Gravel edition, Vol. 3, p. 257.
62. It was signed on 31 August 1965. See Jackson, loc. cit., n. 17.
63. See *War for the Asking,* by Michael Sexton, Penguin 1981.

64. Extracted from an interview in *Vietnam: The New Zealand Story, Part I, Decision.* Produced by Television New Zealand.
65. Ibid.
66. Sexton, op. cit., pp. 91-3.
67. Ibid., pp. 104-5.
68. Ibid., pp. 148, 152.
69. Ibid., p. 171.
70. *The Pentagon Papers*, Senator Gravel edition, Vol. 4, p. 469.
71. Ibid., Vol. 4, p. 470.
72. Figures supplied by Defence Headquarters, Wellington.
73. *The Pentagon Papers*, Senator Gravel edition, Vol. 4, p. 523.
74. Ibid., Vol. 4, p. 239.
75. Ibid., Vol. 4, p. 251.
76. (1965) AJHR A14, p. 69.
77. (1954) 303 NZPD 211 (6 July 1954).
78. 8 July 1954; (1954) 303 NZPD 302.
79. Ibid. The Korean Conflict, however, is not a perfect example of the exercise by the Security Council of its enforcement powers under Chapter VII of the Charter. The action was, admittedly, in the name of the United Nations but it was under United States command. Further, the resolutions enabling the intervention were only passed because of the absence of the Soviet Union from the Council at that time, and even then were only recommendations creating no binding obligations. Some commentators have suggested that it was not a United Nations force at all, merely a group of national forces acting on the recommendation of the Security Council. But it is possible to bring the recommendations within the scope of Article 39. Typically, the Council itself did not indicate which Article it was relying on, but during the debate the United Kingdom pointed out that Article 39 would be appropriate. From the point of view of the states contributing forces the action could be justified either as an exercise of the rights of collective self-defence under Article 51, or as being authorised by the Security Council.
80. (1954) 304 NZPD 1047.
81. Ibid., pp. 1355-6.
82. Ibid., pp. 2100-1.
83. Ibid., p. 2101.
84. See particularly the Preamble and Article III.
85. *The Pentagon Papers*, Senator Gravel edition, Vol. 1, p. 212.
86. See 81 Harv. LR 1771, 1800 (1968). Also J.G. Starke, *The ANZUS*

Treaty Alliance (1965), pp. 118-9.
87. See 81 Harv. LR.
88. See, for example, Eliot D. Hawkins, in *The Vietnam War and International Law*, ed. R.A. Falk, Vol. 1, p. 170.
89. (1965) 342 NZPD 21, see infra at p. 17. But see also the comments of Walter Nash (1954) 304 NZPD 2106 for the view that unanimous consent for armed intervention was required by Article IV(1).
90. Eliot D. Hawkins, loc. cit., p. 171.
91. (1954) 304 NZPD, 201.
92. The ANZUS Treaty, Article IV reads:
'Each Party recognizes that an armed attack in the Pacific Area on any of the Parties would be dangerous to its own peace and safety and declares that it would act to meet the common danger in accordance with its constitutional processes . . . .'
93. The Monroe Doctrine was based on a position taken unilaterally by the United States during the nineteenth century to the effect that an attack on any part of the American continent would threaten the security of the United States and would justify an action in individual self-defence. President Monroe used the words 'dangerous to our peace and safety'. The same notion was enshrined in the Covenant of the League of Nations, Article 21, and was later extended, at Dulles' instigation, to the Organisation of American States: see Greig, op. cit., p. 767 and p. 898;
94. Greig, op.cit., p. 898. It is recognised, of course, that there is a distinction between a unilateral statement, such as the Monroe Doctrine, and a multilateral agreement, such as the SEATO Treaty. Nevertheless, the American ideology which gave rise to the Monroe Doctrine is arguably present in the underlying philosophy of the Manila Treaty.
95. (1954) 304 NZPD 2101-2.
96. Ibid., 2102.
97. Ibid.
98. Ibid.
99. See, for example, (1965) 342 NZPD 10.
100. Mr Webb tried to make the best of it by telling the House ' . . . it could be done through SEATO but so far as New Zealand at any rate is concerned there is no purpose in resorting to that channel when we already have the Colombo Plan and the plan for technical assistance through which we provide financial, economic, and technical aid not only to the nations that are parties to this treaty, but also to other territories in the area'. See (1954) 304 NZPD 2101.

101. For a comprehensive collection of writings on the legality of the war in general, see *The Vietnam War and International Law* three volumes, ed. Richard A. Falk.
102. D.W. Greig, *International Law*, 2nd ed., p. 877.
103. 29 BFSP 1137-8; 30 BFSP 195-6.
104. *Oppenheim's International Law* ed. Lauterpacht, 7th ed. Vol. 2, pp. 155-6.
105. See Bowett, *Self-Defence in International Law,* p. 241; and Kelsen, *The Law of the United Nations*, p. 792.
106. Bowett, op.cit., Chapter X.
107. Ibid., p. 202.
108. Ibid., p. 204. And see Stone, *Legal Controls of International Conflict* p. 264.
109. Bowett, op.cit., p. 205.
110. Ibid., p. 207.
111. North Atlantic Treaty, Article 5.
112. See Akehurst, *A Modern Introduction to International Law* 4th ed. p. 225.
113. Bowett, op.cit., p. 207.
114. See the Declaration of Lima, 1938; and the Act of Habana concerning the Provincial Administration of European Colonies and Possessions in the Americas, 1940.
115. UKTS 29 (1929), Cmnd. 3410; 94 LNTS 57. This treaty is sometimes known as the Pact of Paris, or the Briand-Kellogg Pact.
116. Cited in Bowett, op.cit., p. 212.
117. See Bowett, op.cit., p. 213 and n.1, where he cites, *inter alia*, Wehberg *The Outlawing of War*, p. 86.
118. Bowett, op.cit., p. 215.
119. See Chapter VII of the Charter, esp. Articles 39 and 42.
120. The meaning of the word 'interest' in Article 51 has been the subject of considerable scholarly debate. Some writers have argued that the Article embodies the only right of self-defence now available to Members of the United Nations: see Kelsen, *The Law of the United Nations*, p. 914; Brownlie, *International Law and the Use of Force by States*, pp. 272-5. Others, however, argue that Article 51 leaves a residual right of self-defence under customary international law: see Bowett, *Self-Defence in International Law,* p. 185. The matter has not been resolved.
121. Although Article 2(4) probably states a more general principle of international law which would be binding.
122. See Kelsen, *Recent Trends in the Law of the United Nations*, p. 916.

123. In this sense, it may reflect a conviction that the principles of Article 2 have a general validity in international law beyond the Charter.
124. Eliot D. Hawkins in *The Vietnam War and International Law* ed. Falk, Vol. 1, pp. 167-8. See also Schachter (1948) BYBIL, 115-22.
125. Kelsen, loc.cit., p. 916.
126. Ibid; and see also Kelsen, *The Law of the United Nations*, pp. 791ff.
127. Bowett, op.cit., Chapter X.
128. Ibid., p. 216.
129. Kelsen, *The Law of the United Nations*, pp. 795-6.
130. Bowett, loc.cit. And see, esp. UN Charter, Article 53.
131. Ibid., p. 241.
132. Under the Uniting for Peace Resolution (1950) G.A.R. 377 (V).
133. Indeed, it is doubtful whether the Uniting for Peace Resolution could authorise a regional group to act as such. The wording of the Resolution is that 'the General Assembly shall consider the matter immediately with a view to making appropriate recommendations *to Members* for collective action . . .' (emphasis added). Regional groups are made up (or may be made up) of Members, but are not Members in their own right.
134. Bowett, op.cit., p. 238.
135. (1954) 304 NZPD 2102.
136. For example, New Zealand's Minister of External Affairs (1954) 304 NZPD 2101-2; ibid. 210; ibid. 838.
137. Ibid., p. 210.
138. See Kelsen, *The Law of the United Nations*, pp. 795-6.
139. 54 State Department Bulletin p. 346 at 349 (No. 1393, March 7, 1966).
140. (1965) 342 NZPD 21.
141. Article V. See also the memorandum headed 'The Legality of United States Participation in the Defence of Viet-Nam', March 4, 1966.
142. Brierly, *The Law of Nations*, pp. 395-6.
143. The United States considered that 'armed attack' meant the same thing under the SEATO Treaty as under the Charter. See also Daniel G. Partan, 'Legal Aspects of the Vietnam Conflict', in Falk. op.cit., Vol. 1, p. 232.
144. See D.W. Greig, *International Law*, 2nd ed., p. 907.
145. See Akehurst, (1973) 3 OLR 39 at 43.
146. 'Legality Memorandum' referred to in n.141, above, at para. C. 1.
147. Greig, op.cit., p. 910. And see the Montevideo Convention on the Rights and Duties of States 1933.
148. See 'Legality Memorandum', para. C. 1. See also Akehurst, loc. cit., pp. 42 and 44.

149. Ibid.
150. Quincy Wright, ASIL Proceedings, 151 (1959).
151. A useful and concise analysis is to be found in Akehurst's article cited in n.145, supra.
152. Ibid., p. 913. For a good survey of the law as it applies to civil war, see *La Guerre civile en droit international,* Christophe Piguet, Université de Lausanne, 1982.
153. Statute of the International Court of Justice, Article 38(1)(c). See also the comments of the ICJ in the *Nuclear Tests* cases ICJ Rep. 1974, 268 (para. 46). See also: UN Charter, Article 2(2); Vienna Convention on the Law of Treaties, Articles 26 and 31(1); 77 AJIL 130 (1983).
154. Article 51 does not contain the peace and safety requirement, but Article IV of the SEATO Treaty does. In this context, there is no conflict between the two provisions, so that Article 51 does not prevail and it is possible to see the SEATO Treaty as extending New Zealand's responsibilities in relation to this war to include the perception of a threat to its own peace and safety. Article IV of the ANZUS Treaty may also have been relevant, although the use there of the words 'Pacific Area' does not suggest extension of its scope to the Asian mainland, and this interpretation is borne out by reference to the *travaux préparatoires.* See Starke, *The ANZUS Treaty Alliance* 1965, pp. 48-9.
155. Response to a letter from the author under the Official Information Act to the Ministry of Defence. Reply dated 10 July 1984, DSS/4/16.
156. See Greig, op.cit., p. 916.
157. See Chapter 2, infra.
158. For an opinion that international law itself failed in Vietnam, see Akehurst, loc.cit., n.145 supra.

Index

Agreement on the cessation of hostilities in Vietnam, 10-11, 29
ANZUS Council, 13
ANZUS Treaty, 45
Australia
    American fears for, 22
    commitment of troops to S. Vietnam, 24
    military support by New Zealand, 17
    national security of, 23-4
Bowett, D.W., 37, 38, 39, 42, 43, 44, 45, 54
Bundy, William, 21, 23, 24, 25
Caroline case, The, 36
Civil War, 10, 52, 53
Clifford, Clark, 26
Collective defence, 15-6, 36
    New Zealand's right in S. Vietnam, 54-5
Collective security, 13, 14
Colombo Plan, 47
Demilitarised Zone, 10
Domino theory, 46
Dulles, John Foster, 29
France, 9-12
    surrenders at Dien Bien Phu, 10
    Vietnam, Associate State within, 10
General Assembly (UN), 15, 16
    peacekeeping role of, 44

General principles of law, 53
General Treaty for the Renunciation of War 1928, 38
Geneva Conference, 10
    Agreement on Cessation of Hostilities, 10-11, 29, 50
    Final Declaration, 10-11
    International Control Commission, 10-11
Good Faith
    of New Zealand in Vietnam War, 47, 53, 54
    requirement of in International Law, 53
Greig, D.W., 51
Hanan, Hon. J.R., NZ Attorney-General, 16, 17
    views of SEATO Treaty, 17-8
Holyoake, Rt. Hon. K.J., NZ Prime Minister, 13, 14, 16, 33
Hazlett, Luke, 24
Indonesian Archipelago, fears for, 22
International Control Commission, 10-11
Johnson, Lyndon B.
    as Vice-President, 19
    as President, 15, 22, 25
Katzenbach, Nicholas deB., 25
Kelsen, Hans, 42, 43

Kennedy, President John F., 19
Korea, 20, 28
Lodge, Henry Cabot, 23
Manila Conference, 28, 33
Manila nations, US memo concerning, 25
Manila Treaty: see South East Asia Collective Defence Treaty
Marshall, Rt. Hon. John, NZ Deputy Prime Minister, 16, 17, 24
McNamara, Robert, 20, 21, 25
Monroe Doctrine, 31, 32, 34, 38
Munro, Sir Leslie, 19, 23
NAFTA Agreement, 23
National Liberation Front (NLF), 11, 12, 50, 51
North Atlantic Treaty Organisation (NATO), 21, 28
    Treaty compared with SEATO's, 30, 34, 37, 42
Operation Rolling Thunder, 15
Organisation of American States (OAS), 21
Peacekeeping, 13, 14, 15, 33
Pentagon Papers, 21, 29
Quat, Dr., Prime Minister of S. Vietnam, 14
Regional defence and UN Charter, 43, 44-5, 48
Rostow, Walt W., 25
Rusk, Dean, 20, 21, 25, 47
Security Council
    advised of NZ involvement in S. Vietnam, 9, 13, 39, 55
    and collective self-defence, 42, 44, 55
    duty to report to under SEATO Treaty, 33
    veto, 16, 44

Self-defence, 35-8, 54-5
    inherent right to, 39-40
Sexton, Michael, 23, 24
South East Asia Collective Defence Treaty
    Preamble, 33
    Article I, 33
    Article III, 32
    Article IV, 29, 56
    Article IV(1), 17, 30, 31, 33, 37 48
    Article IV(2), 17, 32
    Article IV(3), 56
    compared with North Atlantic Treaty, 30, 34, 37, 42
    New Zealand view of, 17-8
    requirement of unanimity, 47, 48
    signature, 28
    United States Protocol to, 31, 45-6
South East Asia Treaty Organisation (SEATO)
    and collective defence, 15, 16
    Council, support for S. Vietnam, 16, 17
    effectiveness of, 19-20
    lack of British and French support, 19, 20
    reasons for formation of, 27-9
Sovereign equality, doctrine of, 35
Soviet Union
    complaint to Security Council, 9
    protest to New Zealand, 9
Statehood of N. and S. Vietnam, 51
Thailand, fears for, 22
Troop strengths in Vietnam, 25
United Nations
    peacekeeping, 15, 33
    impotence of, 14, 15, 33
United Nations Charter

Article 2(3), 39
Article 2(4), 39, 40, 41, 55
Article 2(6), 40
Article 43(3), 30
Article 51, 39, 40, 41, 43, 44, 45, 47, 48, 49, 55, 56, 57
Article 52(1), 44, 47
Article 53, 44
Article 54, 43
Article 103, 41, 55
collective defence and, 16

regional defence and, 44
self-defence and, 13, 36, 38, 39
use of force under, 36, 39
Viet Cong, 12, 13
Viet Minh
    recognised by Soviety Union and China, 9
    war against French, 10
Webb, Hon. T.C., NZ Minister of External Affairs, 27, 28, 29, 30, 31, 32, 33